Different Companies

Paulette Durand

Copyright Page

Index

The New Business Paradigm

In recent decades, we have witnessed a radical transformation in the way businesses are conceived and managed. What once worked as a sure recipe for success today seems obsolete or insufficient. The rules of the game have changed, and with them, the mentality and expectations of leaders, employees and consumers alike. This new business paradigm not only redefines how companies operate, but also the very purpose of their existence. It is no longer just about generating profits; It is about generating impact, both in society and on the planet.

Traditionally, companies have focused on maximizing economic profits, and although this remains an important part of the business, today it is not enough. Society is demanding more from corporations. Consumers prefer to support brands that align with their values, that are transparent, ethical and responsible. This change in expectations has forced companies to rethink their role in the world. They can no longer operate as isolated entities focused solely on their own interests; They must be considered key actors in building a better future.

This new business paradigm is based on three fundamental pillars: innovation, sustainability and purpose. Innovation is no longer just an engine of growth; It is an imperative. Companies that do not innovate risk being left behind in a world that changes at a dizzying pace. However, it is not about innovating for the sake of it, but about innovating with a clear purpose. Technology, for example, should not be adopted simply because it is fashionable, but because it can improve people's lives, make processes more efficient or reduce environmental impact. The companies of the future must be willing to question what is established, to experiment and learn from their mistakes to stay relevant and competitive.

Sustainability, on the other hand, has ceased to be an option and has become a necessity. In a world where natural resources are finite and climate change is an unavoidable reality, companies must adopt sustainable practices to ensure their long-term survival. This means not only reducing their carbon footprint or recycling more, but also completely rethinking their business models so that they are regenerative – that is, they give back more than they take. Companies that manage to integrate sustainability into their DNA will not only gain consumer loyalty, but will also be better positioned to meet the challenges of the future.

Purpose is the third pillar of this new paradigm. The companies that will thrive in the future will be those that have a clear and meaningful purpose, one that goes beyond simply generating profits. This purpose must be authentic, resonate with the company's values, and be evident in every aspect of its operation. A purpose-driven company will not only attract consumers, but will also inspire its employees, generating greater engagement and productivity. Workers, especially the younger generations, are looking for more than just a paycheck; They want to feel part of something bigger, something that has a positive impact on the world.

This shift towards an approach based on innovation, sustainability and purpose is not just a fad; It is a response to the needs and demands of a constantly evolving world. Companies that do not adapt to this new paradigm risk becoming irrelevant, while those that embrace it will have the opportunity to lead the change and build a lasting legacy.

The new business paradigm also demands a change in leadership mindset. Today's leaders can no longer be autocratic, focused solely on control and efficiency. They must be visionaries, able to inspire and motivate their teams, and be willing to listen, learn and evolve. This transformational leadership is critical to guiding companies through uncertainty and into a future full of possibilities.

In conclusion, the new business paradigm calls us to rethink the reason for being of companies, to adopt a broader vision and to take actions that generate a positive impact on the world. It is a call to action for all those who want to build different companies, companies that not only survive, but thrive in a world that demands more. Innovation, sustainability and purpose are not just buzzwords; They are the foundations on which the companies of the future will be built. As we move forward, those companies that manage to integrate these elements into their essence will be the ones that lead the way, not only towards economic success, but also towards a more just, equitable and sustainable world.

Paulette Durand

Culture as a Central Pillar

When we talk about what makes a company truly different, the first place we should look is its culture. Company culture is the heart and soul of any organization. It is the set of values, beliefs and behaviors that define how things are done within the company. It's what brings employees together and shapes how they interact with each other, with customers, and with the outside world. In short, culture is the central pillar on which everything else is built.

In a traditional company, culture is often taken for granted, a natural consequence of how things have been done over time. However, in a company that aspires to be different, culture cannot be left to chance. It must be designed and cultivated with intention, because a strong, positive culture not only drives performance, but is also the foundation upon which all other strategies can be implemented.

Imagine a company as a garden. If you only focus on the results, that is, on the flowers and fruits, you can miss the most important thing: caring for the soil and roots. Company culture is that fertile soil that allows everything else to grow and flourish. Without a strong culture, any attempt at innovation, sustainability or leadership is doomed to fail, because there is no fertile ground for those ideas to thrive.

A strong company culture starts with a clear set of values. These values should be authentic and reflect what the company really believes, not just what sounds good in a press release. For example, if a company says it values innovation, then it must be willing to take risks, accept failure as part of the process, and encourage creativity at all levels. If you say you value sustainability, then you should make environmental responsibility a priority in all of your operations. These values are not just words; They are principles that guide daily decisions and are reflected in each action.

But values alone are not enough. For a culture to truly work, those values must be lived and breathed by everyone in the organization, from the CEO to the newest employee. This requires leadership that not only speaks of those values, but exemplifies them in its behavior. Leaders are the gardeners of culture; They are responsible for nurturing it, protecting it, and making sure everyone understands and respects it.

A positive company culture is also inclusive and diverse. Companies that value diversity of thought, experience and perspective are the best equipped to innovate and adapt to change. Diversity is not just about meeting quotas, but about creating an environment where all voices are heard and valued. When people feel that they can be themselves at work, that their ideas are appreciated, and that they have the freedom to contribute fully, the company benefits from greater creativity, collaboration, and loyalty.

Another key aspect of a strong culture is transparency. Transparency fosters trust, and trust is essential to any relationship, including work relationships. When employees feel that information is shared openly and decisions are made fairly, it creates a sense of belonging and commitment. On the contrary, a culture of secrecy and opacity only leads to mistrust, discontent and, ultimately, demotivation.

Flexibility is also crucial in a different company culture. The world is changing rapidly, and companies must be willing to adapt. This means being open to new ways of working, such as remote work or flexible hours, and being willing to reexamine and adjust practices and policies when necessary. A rigid culture, which clings to "this is how we've always done it," is destined to be left behind.

Furthermore, a company culture focused on well-being is a culture that thrives. When employees feel that their physical, emotional, and mental health is a priority for the company, it creates a more positive and productive work environment. This can range from wellness programs and mental health benefits to simply encouraging a healthy work-life balance. Companies that care about the well-being of their employees not only reduce absenteeism and burnout, but also increase staff satisfaction and retention.

Finally, a strong culture should be constantly celebrated and reinforced. Companies must find ways to recognize and reward behaviors that reflect their values.

This not only keeps the culture alive, but also motivates employees to continue aligning with those values. Celebrations don't have to be grand; Sometimes a simple thank you or public recognition can have a big impact.

In conclusion, company culture is not just another aspect of the company; It is the central pillar that supports everything else. It is the foundation on which innovation, sustainability and leadership are built. A strong, positive and inclusive culture not only improves performance and productivity, but also creates an environment where people want to work, collaborate and grow. Companies that understand the importance of culture and cultivate it with intention are better positioned to be different, to stand out in a saturated market, and to successfully lead into the future.

Paulette Durand

Transformative Leadership

At the heart of every successful company, you will always find strong leadership, but in a different company, that leadership is not only strong, it is transformative. Transformational leadership goes beyond simply managing people and resources; It's about inspiring, motivating and guiding a team towards a future full of possibilities. This type of leadership is not about controlling every aspect of the business, but rather about creating an environment where people feel empowered to do their best.

Traditional leadership, which is based on authority and power, is being replaced by a more humane and empathetic approach. Instead of telling people what to do, transformational leaders invite them to participate in creating a shared vision. This type of leader is a guide, mentor, and facilitator who helps their team reach their full potential. Instead of being the one with all the answers, he is the one asking the right questions and encouraging critical thinking.

One of the main characteristics of transformational leadership is the ability to inspire. Inspiring doesn't mean giving motivational speeches every day, but rather living the company's values and vision in a way that motivates others to follow suit. Transformational leaders understand that their actions speak louder than their words. When a leader shows commitment, passion and authenticity, the team feels it and reflects it in their own work. To inspire is to spread that sense of purpose that makes work have meaning beyond simply completing tasks.

Another essential characteristic of transformational leadership is empathy. Transformational leaders genuinely care about the people they lead. They understand that each team member is a human being with their own challenges, dreams and needs. This empathy translates into leadership that listens, cares, and is willing to support their team through difficult times. A leader who practices empathy creates an environment of trust and respect, where employees feel valued and understood. This human connection is essential to building a strong and cohesive company culture.

Transformational leadership also relies on the ability to foster personal growth and development. Leaders who take this approach view each team member as a long-term investment. Instead of just focusing on short-term performance, they care about each person's skill development, continuous learning, and professional growth. This can include training opportunities, mentoring, and challenges that take employees out of their comfort zone so they can reach new heights. A transformational leader celebrates individual and collective successes, and recognizes that each person's growth contributes to the overall success of the company.

Authenticity is another cornerstone of transformational leadership. Authentic leaders are those who are true to themselves and their values, and who do not try to be something they are not. This authenticity is conveyed in every interaction and decision they make. They do not try to hide their weaknesses, but rather they recognize them and work on them, which makes them more human and accessible. When a leader is authentic, he creates an environment where others also feel comfortable being themselves, which encourages diversity of thought and innovation.

Furthermore, a transformational leader does not fear change; He hugs him and drives him. He understands that change is a constant in the business world and that adapting quickly is crucial to long-term success. Instead of resisting new ideas or clinging to old ways of doing things, these leaders actively look for ways to innovate and improve. They are willing to take calculated risks and learn from failures, knowing that every mistake is an opportunity to grow and improve. This growth mindset is what drives a different company to stay ahead in a constantly evolving environment.

Vision is another key component of transformational leadership. Leaders with vision have a clear picture of where they want to take their company and how they plan to get there. This vision is not just a list of goals to achieve, but an inspiring narrative that motivates the entire team to work together toward a common purpose. A transformational leader shares this vision clearly and consistently, ensuring that each team member understands their role in achieving that future. Additionally, it ensures that the vision is not only focused on financial success, but also on the positive impact the company can have on society and the environment.

Transformational leadership also manifests itself in the ability to make difficult decisions with courage and compassion. Leaders often face situations where there are no easy answers, and the decisions they make can have a significant impact on the lives of their employees and the future of the company. A transformative leader does not run away from these responsibilities, but neither does he take them lightly. He evaluates all options, considers potential consequences, and makes informed decisions that align with the company's values and vision. And most importantly, he communicates openly and honestly with his team, explaining the reasons behind each decision and offering support to those who may be affected.

Finally, transformational leadership is about creating a legacy. Transformational leaders don't just think about short-term success, but about the lasting impact they want to leave. They are committed to building something that lasts, something that will continue to thrive long after they are gone. This legacy can be a strong company culture, a meaningful mission, or a community of employees who are proud of their work. A transformational leader works tirelessly to ensure that their company not only survives, but thrives and continues to make a difference in the world.

In short, transformational leadership is the engine that drives a different company. It is leadership that inspires, that cares about the well-being and growth of people, that is authentic and visionary. It is leadership that is not afraid of change, that makes difficult decisions with compassion and that focuses on creating a lasting legacy. Companies that have transformational leaders are better equipped to face the challenges of the future, to innovate and to lead with purpose. In a world where change is the only constant, transformational leadership is what separates successful companies from those that fall behind.

Disruptive Innovation

Innovation is the lifeblood of any company that wants to be different, but disruptive innovation is the type of innovation that truly changes the rules of the game. It's not just about improving an existing product or service, but creating something completely new that transforms entire industries, changes the way people live or work, or opens doors to possibilities that previously seemed impossible. Disruptive innovation doesn't just improve what already exists; replaces it or reinvents it in a way that makes the previous obsolete.

To understand disruptive innovation, let's think about some examples that have changed the world. Consider how Netflix revolutionized the entertainment industry. Before Netflix, people were used to going to a video rental store, like Blockbuster, to rent movies. But Netflix didn't just make movies available online; completely changed the way people consume entertainment, introducing streaming and allowing users to watch what they wanted, whenever they wanted. This disruptive approach not only affected video rental stores, but also forced the film and television industry to adapt to a new model.

Another clear example is that of smartphones. Before the iPhone, cell phones were primarily for making calls and sending text messages. Apple, with its disruptive innovation, not only created a new type of device, but radically changed how we interact with technology and the world around us. The iPhone combined a phone, a camera, an Internet browser, and many other features into a single device, creating a whole new category and leaving traditional phones behind.

These examples show that disruptive innovation is not just about being better, but about being completely different. But how is this achieved? The first step is to think boldly and not be afraid to challenge the status quo. Companies that focus on disruptive innovation are not content with making incremental improvements; They seek to change the rules of the game. This requires a mindset that is willing to take risks, fail, and learn quickly from those failures.

The second key ingredient for disruptive innovation is the ability to identify unmet needs or unsolved problems in the market. Many of the most disruptive innovations have arisen from the ability to see a need that no one else had identified or to find a new way to address a problem that everyone had assumed had no solution. This requires a deep understanding of customers and how their needs and wants are evolving over time.

For example, Airbnb emerged because the founders saw that many people were looking for more accessible and personalized forms of accommodation when they traveled. Instead of creating a new type of hotel, they realized that many people would be willing to rent their houses or rooms to travelers. This concept was completely disruptive, and changed the way people think about accommodation, creating a whole new industry in the process.

Technology also plays a crucial role in disruptive innovation. Often the most disruptive innovations are enabled by new technologies that allow companies to do things that were not possible before. However, simply adopting the latest technology is not enough; It is necessary to think about how that technology can be used in new and creative ways to solve problems or create value. This requires an open mindset and a willingness to experiment and try new things.

Company culture is another important factor. Companies that foster a culture of innovation are better positioned to be disruptive. This means creating an environment where people feel safe to express ideas, take risks, and experiment without fear of failure. Instead of punishing failure, innovative companies see it as an opportunity to learn and improve. Additionally, a culture of innovation values collaboration and diversity of thought, recognizing that the best ideas often emerge from the combination of different perspectives and skills.

But disruptive innovation isn't just for big companies with big budgets. In fact, many of the most disruptive innovations have emerged from small startups that had no choice but to think creatively and do more with less. These small businesses often have the advantage of being agile and less tied to traditional processes, allowing them to move quickly and adapt to changes in the market. However, large companies can also be disruptive if they are willing to adopt a startup mentality and foster innovation at all levels of the organization.

It is important to note that disruptive innovation is not always welcomed at first. In fact, many disruptive innovations have been initially rejected or criticized because they challenge the status quo and demand a change in mindset. However, disruptive innovators understand that change takes time and are willing to persevere despite initial difficulties. They know that if their innovation truly solves a problem or meets a need in a new and better way, it will eventually find its place in the market.

Once a disruptive innovation begins to gain traction, it can have a ripple effect, changing not only the company or industry that introduced it, but also other related industries and sectors. For example, the introduction of the electric car has not only changed the automotive industry, but has also had an impact on the energy industry, urban infrastructure and environmental policies. This is the power of disruptive innovation: it can have a broad and lasting impact that goes beyond its origin.

In conclusion, disruptive innovation is the type of innovation that truly transforms and redefines entire industries. It's not just about doing things better, but about doing them completely differently. It requires a bold mindset, a culture that encourages experimentation and learning, and a willingness to challenge the status quo. Companies seeking to be truly different must adopt disruptive innovation as a core strategy, as it is the key to leading change, creating new opportunities and building a future that previously seemed impossible. In a world where change is constant, the ability to be disruptive is not just an advantage, it is a necessity.

Technology and Digitalization

We live in an era where technology has ceased to be a simple tool and has become the core of almost everything we do. In companies, technology is no longer a luxury, but a fundamental necessity to compete and prosper. But when we talk about a different company, one of those that are designed for the future, technology and digitalization are not only important pieces; They are the foundation on which everything else is built. Technology and digitalization allow companies to be more agile, efficient and innovative, and those that do not adapt to this new reality risk being left behind.

To understand the impact of technology on business, it is useful to think about how it has transformed our daily lives. Not long ago, if you wanted to buy something, you had to go to a physical store. Today, with just a few clicks on your phone, you can buy almost anything from anywhere in the world and have it delivered to your doorstep in a matter of days. This change has been made possible by technology, which has revolutionized the way we shop, work, communicate and live in general.

In the business world, digitalization refers to the use of digital technologies to transform processes, improve efficiency and create new business opportunities. For example, instead of manually keeping track of sales on a sheet of paper, a company can use management software that not only records sales but also analyzes the data to identify trends, forecast demand, and optimize sales. inventory. This type of digitization not only saves time and reduces errors, but also provides valuable information that can help the company make more informed and strategic decisions.

Technology also allows companies to automate routine and repetitive tasks, freeing employees to focus on activities that truly add value. For example, instead of an employee spending hours entering data into a spreadsheet, automation software can do that job in minutes, error-free. This not only increases productivity, but also improves employee morale as they can dedicate their time to more creative and rewarding tasks.

But digitalization is not just about efficiency. It also opens up new possibilities for innovation and customization. In the past, companies offered products and services that were essentially the same to all customers. But with technology, it is now possible to personalize each customer's experience, tailoring products and services to their individual needs and preferences. This not only improves customer satisfaction, but also creates loyalty and fosters long-term relationships.

A clear example of how digitalization has transformed the customer experience is the use of algorithms on platforms such as Netflix or Amazon. These algorithms analyze your viewing or purchasing habits to recommend movies, series or products that you will probably like. This personalization is possible thanks to technology and has completely changed the way we interact with these platforms. Now, companies not only offer a product or service, but a unique experience adapted to each user.

Technology has also changed the way companies communicate, both internally and with their customers. Previously, companies relied on in-person meetings, phone calls or emails to communicate. Today, tools like Slack, Microsoft Teams or Zoom have revolutionized communication, allowing teams to collaborate in real time from anywhere in the world. These tools not only facilitate communication, but also encourage greater collaboration and creativity by allowing ideas to flow more freely and spontaneously.

Furthermore, digitalization has opened the door to new business models. Companies like Uber or Airbnb would not exist without digital technology that allows them to connect millions of users with drivers or homeowners in real time. These business models have changed entire industries, proving that technology not only improves what already exists, but can also create something completely new.

However, the adoption of technology and digitalization is not without challenges. One of the biggest obstacles is resistance to change. Many companies, especially larger, more established ones, tend to stick with their old ways of doing things because they are comfortable or because that's how they've always worked. But in a world where technology advances at a dizzying pace, this mentality is dangerous. Companies that are not willing to adapt and adopt new technologies run the risk of being left behind and losing relevance in the market.

Another challenge is cybersecurity. As companies go digital, they become more vulnerable to cyberattacks and data breaches. Protecting sensitive customer and company information is a critical priority in a digital world. This requires not only investments in security technology, but also creating a culture of cybersecurity awareness throughout the organization. All employees must be trained to identify and prevent potential threats, and the company must be prepared to respond quickly in the event of an incident.

Furthermore, digitalization raises questions about ethics and privacy. As companies collect and analyze more data about their customers, it is essential that they do so responsibly and respectfully. This is not only important to comply with regulations, but also to maintain customer trust. Companies need to be transparent about how they use data and ensure it is protected and used in ways that benefit customers, not just the company.

In conclusion, technology and digitalization are fundamental drivers for any company that aspires to be different and relevant in the future. They are not just tools to improve efficiency; They are means to transform the way we do business, interact with customers and create value. However, to make the most of these opportunities, companies must be willing to embrace change, invest in cybersecurity, and act responsibly in handling data. In a digital world, the ability to adapt and evolve with technology is not only a competitive advantage; It is a necessity for long-term survival and success. Companies that understand this and put technology and digitalization at the center of their strategy are better positioned to lead in an ever-changing market and to build a strong, sustainable future.

Paulette Durand

Sustainability as a Strategic Axis

Sustainability is no longer a buzzword or an option for companies; has become a strategic imperative. In a world where natural resources are finite and environmental concerns are increasingly urgent, companies that do not incorporate sustainability at the heart of their strategy risk becoming obsolete. Being sustainable does not only mean taking care of the environment, but also creating a business model that can last over time, that is responsible with its resources and that has a positive impact on society.

To understand the importance of sustainability, it is useful to consider how companies have operated in the past. For decades, many companies focused almost exclusively on maximizing short-term profits, often at the expense of the environment and communities. This meant exploiting natural resources without thinking about the long-term consequences, generating massive amounts of waste and carbon emissions, and contributing to climate change in significant ways. However, this approach is unsustainable. Not only because it damages the planet, but because it also puts the company's own future at risk.

Companies that adopt sustainability as a strategic axis understand that their long-term success is intrinsically linked to the well-being of the planet and society. This means that they not only seek to generate profits, but do so in a way that is compatible with respect for the environment and people. Sustainability thus becomes a competitive advantage, since consumers, increasingly aware and concerned about these issues, tend to prefer products and services from companies that demonstrate a real commitment to sustainability.

One of the most direct ways companies can be sustainable is by managing their resources responsibly. This means reducing the consumption of energy, water and raw materials, and seeking renewable and recycled sources whenever possible. For example, a company that manufactures products may choose to use recycled materials instead of virgin raw materials, or may invest in technologies that reduce water consumption in its production process. These practices not only help preserve natural resources, but can also reduce long-term costs and improve operational efficiency.

Another key area of sustainability is waste management. For too long, companies have produced large amounts of waste that ends up in landfills or, worse, in our oceans and ecosystems. But a sustainable company seeks to reduce, reuse and recycle this waste. An example of this is the concept of the circular economy, where products at the end of their useful life are not thrown away, but are returned to the production cycle as new resources. This not only reduces the amount of waste, but also promotes innovation and efficiency in the use of resources.

Sustainability also extends to the supply chain. Companies cannot be considered truly sustainable if their suppliers do not follow responsible practices. Therefore, a company that takes sustainability seriously works closely with its suppliers to ensure that they are also committed to responsible resource management, respect for human rights and minimizing environmental impact. This can include everything from making sure materials come from certified sources to requiring fair working conditions in your suppliers' factories.

Sustainability not only refers to the environment, but also social impact. A sustainable company cares about the well-being of its employees, its customers and the communities in which it operates. This involves paying fair wages, providing safe and healthy working conditions, and contributing to the development of local communities through initiatives such as education, health and job creation. It also means being transparent and ethical in all your operations, and acting with integrity in all business relationships.

Additionally, sustainable companies strive to minimize their carbon footprint, recognizing the crucial role they play in the fight against climate change. This may involve adopting renewable energy, such as solar or wind, rather than relying on fossil fuels. It may also include the implementation of energy efficiency policies, such as improving building efficiency, using low-consumption technologies, and reducing emissions in logistics and transportation. Some companies even commit to being "carbon neutral," meaning they offset all of their carbon emissions by investing in projects that absorb or reduce carbon, such as reforestation or renewable energy.

Another important aspect of sustainability is innovation. Companies that prioritize sustainability are constantly looking for new ways of doing things, developing products and services that are less harmful to the environment or that help solve social and environmental problems. For example, many companies are investing in the development of biodegradable products, recyclable packaging or solutions that promote energy efficiency. Sustainability, in this sense, is not a barrier to innovation, but rather a source of new ideas and opportunities.

In addition to the environmental and social benefits, sustainability also makes strong economic sense. Companies that adopt sustainable practices often find that these can lead to significant savings and the creation of new revenue streams. For example, by reducing energy and material consumption, companies can reduce their operating costs. Likewise, by developing sustainable products, they can access new markets and attract consumers who are willing to pay more for products that align with their values.

However, sustainability is not something that can be achieved overnight. It requires long-term commitment and a strategic approach. Companies must integrate sustainability into all areas of their business, from strategic planning to daily decision making. This may require changes to organizational culture, new investments in technology and processes, and greater collaboration with all stakeholders, including employees, suppliers, customers, and the broader community.

Communication is also key to sustainability. Companies must be transparent about their sustainability efforts and progress, informing their customers and the general public about what they are doing and why. This transparency not only builds trust, but can also inspire other companies to follow suit and consumers to make more informed decisions. Companies that communicate effectively about their commitment to sustainability can also differentiate themselves in the market and build a strong, positive brand.

In summary, sustainability as a strategic axis is essential for any company that aspires to be different and relevant in the future. It is not only a social or environmental responsibility, but an opportunity to innovate, reduce costs, create long-term value and build a strong and lasting relationship with customers and the community. Companies that understand this and put sustainability at the center of their strategy will be better positioned to meet the challenges of the 21st century and to lead with a purpose that goes beyond short-term profits. Sustainability is ultimately an investment in the future, not only of the company, but of the world in which we live.

Paulette Durand

Diversity and Inclusion

Diversity and inclusion are more than just buzzwords; They are fundamental principles to build a truly successful and different company. In a world where cultural, social and economic barriers are being broken down, companies that embrace diversity and inclusion not only better reflect the society in which they operate, but are also better prepared to innovate, adapt and grow. But what do these terms really mean, and why are they so important to business success?

When we talk about diversity, we refer to the presence of different types of people in an organization. This includes, but is not limited to, diversity of gender, race, ethnicity, age, sexual orientation, abilities, experiences and perspectives. In a diverse company, people come from different backgrounds and bring with them a wide range of ideas, approaches and points of view. This diversity enriches the work environment and allows the company to approach problems from multiple angles, often leading to more creative and innovative solutions.

Inclusion, on the other hand, refers to how that diversity is valued and respected within the organization. It is not enough to have a diverse workforce; It is crucial that all people feel valued, heard and empowered to contribute fully. Inclusion means creating an environment where each person can be authentic, where they feel safe to express their ideas, and where their contributions are recognized and appreciated. In an inclusive company, no one feels excluded or marginalized for being different.

The combination of diversity and inclusion is powerful because it not only allows companies to attract and retain top talent, but also improves decision making, innovation and customer satisfaction. When people with different experiences and perspectives come together, innovative ideas that challenge the status quo are more likely to emerge. Additionally, an inclusive environment where all voices are valued fosters greater collaboration and a sense of belonging, which in turn increases employee morale and engagement.

One of the most obvious benefits of diversity and inclusion is the company's ability to better understand and serve a global and diverse customer base. Today's consumers are incredibly diverse, and they expect companies to reflect that diversity. A company with a diverse workforce can better connect with different customer segments, understand their unique needs and preferences, and offer products and services that truly resonate with them. This not only improves customer satisfaction, but can also open up new market opportunities and increase sales.

However, achieving true diversity and inclusion is not an easy task, nor something that will happen overnight. It requires genuine and ongoing commitment from senior management and an organizational culture that values and promotes these principles. One of the first steps is to recognize that we all have unconscious biases that can affect our decisions and behaviors. These biases can influence everything from who we hire to how we evaluate employee performance. It is therefore crucial that companies take proactive measures to identify and mitigate these biases, through training and awareness.

Additionally, it is important to establish policies and practices that promote diversity and inclusion at all levels of the organization. This can include hiring policies that actively seek to attract diverse candidates, mentoring and development programs to support employees from underrepresented groups, and creating affinity groups where employees can connect and support each other. It is also essential to measure and track progress in these areas, to ensure that diversity and inclusion initiatives are having the desired impact.

Inclusion also means giving all employees the tools and resources they need to succeed. This may mean making reasonable accommodations for people with disabilities, providing flexible work options to accommodate different needs and responsibilities, and ensuring everyone has access to professional development opportunities. When employees feel that their company truly cares about their well-being and development, they are more committed and motivated to give their best.

Communication is another key aspect of inclusion. It is important for companies to foster a culture of open and honest communication, where employees feel comfortable sharing their ideas, concerns and suggestions without fear of retaliation. This requires leaders who are willing to actively listen, learn from their employees, and act on what they hear. It also means celebrating differences and recognizing everyone's contributions, reinforcing the idea that each person is valuable and has something unique to offer.

A concrete example of how diversity and inclusion can transform a company is the case of Google. Over the years, Google has worked hard to build an inclusive culture, where diversity of thought is valued and innovation is promoted. They have implemented programs to increase the representation of women and minorities in technology, and have created an environment where everyone's ideas and contributions are valued. This approach has not only allowed Google to attract some of the best talent in the world, but has also helped the company stay at the forefront of technological innovation.

Another important aspect of diversity and inclusion is the positive impact on the company's reputation. Companies that are seen as diverse and inclusive are more attractive to employees, customers and investors. In an increasingly competitive market, having a positive reputation in these areas can be a significant advantage. Employees want to work for companies that respect their values and where they feel they can be themselves. Customers, especially younger generations, prefer brands that reflect their values of diversity and inclusion. And investors are increasingly interested in supporting companies that demonstrate a commitment to social responsibility and inclusion.

However, it is important for companies to address diversity and inclusion authentically. It's not just about meeting a quota or marketing about how well you're doing. Employees and customers can quickly detect when a company is not genuine in its commitment to these values.

Diversity and inclusion should be an integral part of the company's culture and strategy, not something that is added as an extra.

In short, diversity and inclusion are not just good practices; They are essential to the success and sustainability of any company in the modern world. By valuing and taking advantage of differences, companies can be more innovative, adaptable and competitive. Inclusion ensures that all voices are heard and all employees feel valued, which in turn fosters a healthier, more collaborative and productive work environment. Companies that adopt diversity and inclusion as strategic pillars not only better reflect the reality of the society in which they operate, but are also better positioned to thrive in a global and diverse market. Ultimately, diversity and inclusion is not just about doing the right thing, but about doing what is best for the future of the company and society as a whole.

Paulette Durand

Emotional Intelligence in the Company

Emotional intelligence is a concept that has gained a lot of relevance in recent years, and it is not difficult to understand why. In a business environment where technical skills and knowledge are essential, emotional intelligence adds a critical dimension to organizational success. Emotional intelligence, in simple terms, is the ability to understand, manage and use emotions, both your own and others, in a constructive way. In a world where human interactions are inevitable, and often complex, emotional intelligence becomes an invaluable asset for any company that aspires to be different and prosper in the future.

When we talk about emotional intelligence in the company, we are referring to the ability of employees and leaders to manage their emotions in ways that benefit both themselves and the organization as a whole. This includes the ability to remain calm under pressure, to respond empathetically to the needs and concerns of others, and to make decisions that consider not only rational, but also emotional aspects. In an environment where impulsive or poorly managed decisions can have serious consequences, emotional intelligence offers a more balanced and effective approach.

One of the most important aspects of emotional intelligence is self-awareness. Self-awareness involves understanding our own emotions, recognizing how they influence our thoughts and behaviors, and being aware of our strengths and weaknesses. In the business context, a self-aware employee or leader is able to identify when her emotions may be clouding her judgment or affecting her performance. This ability to introspect allows people to make adjustments in real time, preventing negative emotions from dominating their actions and decisions. Additionally, self-awareness promotes a sense of authenticity and transparency, which strengthens trust and respect in the workplace.

Another crucial component of emotional intelligence is self-management, which is the ability to control one's own emotions and behaviors. In a work environment, it is normal to face stressful situations, conflicts and unforeseen challenges. Self-management allows employees and leaders to maintain composure, think clearly, and respond appropriately, rather than react impulsively. This skill is especially important in leadership roles, where quick and often difficult decisions are part of everyday life. A leader who can manage their emotions effectively is able to make more informed decisions and maintain a positive work environment, even in times of crisis.

Empathy is another pillar of emotional intelligence and is vital in any business environment. Empathy is the ability to put yourself in someone else's shoes, to understand and share the feelings of others. In a company, empathy allows employees and leaders to connect more deeply with their colleagues, customers and partners. This not only improves communication and collaboration, but also helps build stronger, longer-lasting relationships. Empathy is especially important in team management, where understanding employees' needs and concerns can be key to motivating them, resolving conflicts, and creating a more harmonious work environment.

Emotional intelligence also involves social skills, such as the ability to build and maintain effective relationships, to influence others positively, and to manage conflict constructively. In the business context, soft skills are essential for collaboration and teamwork. An employee or leader with strong social skills is able to work well with others, resolve disputes peacefully, and inspire her team to achieve common goals. These skills are especially valuable in an environment where success depends on cooperation and synergy between different individuals and departments.

One of the most important advantages of emotional intelligence in the company is its impact on organizational culture. A company culture that values and promotes emotional intelligence is a culture where people feel valued, understood and supported. This not only improves employee satisfaction and well-being, but also increases productivity and performance. In an environment where emotions are managed effectively, employees are more motivated, more creative, and more committed to the company's goals. Additionally, a culture of emotional intelligence can help attract and retain talent, as employees tend to prefer working in places where they feel emotionally connected and appreciated.

Emotional intelligence also plays a crucial role in decision making. Business decisions often involve a balance between logic and emotion. While data and analytics are critical, how this data is perceived and interpreted can be influenced by our emotions. A leader with high emotional intelligence is able to recognize when her own or others' emotions might be affecting objectivity, and can take steps to ensure that decisions are rational and balanced. Additionally, emotional intelligence allows leaders to consider the emotional impact of their decisions on employees and other stakeholders, which is essential for maintaining a positive and cohesive work environment.

Another area where emotional intelligence is vital is in change management. Change is a constant in the business world, and can often be a source of stress and anxiety for employees. Emotional intelligence allows leaders to manage change in ways that minimize resistance and maximize acceptance. This is achieved through empathetic communication, understanding employees' concerns and fears, and creating a supportive environment where everyone feels part of the change process. An emotionally intelligent leader can guide her team through uncertainty and transition, keeping morale high and ensuring everyone is aligned with the new direction.

Furthermore, emotional intelligence is essential for leadership. Emotionally intelligent leaders are not only capable of managing their own emotions, but they are also experts at managing the emotions of others. This allows them to inspire, motivate and guide their teams effectively. An emotionally intelligent leader knows how to give constructive feedback, how to celebrate successes, and how to support his team through difficult times. These leaders create an environment of trust and respect, where employees feel safe to express their ideas and take risks. Ultimately, leadership based on emotional intelligence is key to building a successful, sustainable and humane company.

Of course, developing emotional intelligence is not something that happens overnight. It requires practice, self-reflection, and a genuine commitment to personal growth. Companies that want to foster emotional intelligence in their organization can offer training and resources to help employees and leaders develop these skills. This may include workshops on stress management, effective communication courses, and mentoring and coaching programs. By investing in the development of emotional intelligence, companies not only improve the well-being of their employees, but also strengthen their ability to face the challenges of the future with resilience and confidence.

In short, emotional intelligence is an essential skill in the modern business world. It goes beyond technical skills and knowledge, and focuses on the ability to understand and manage emotions effectively. By fostering self-awareness, self-management, empathy and social skills, emotional intelligence enables people and businesses to thrive in an increasingly complex and dynamic environment. It is a powerful tool to improve decision making, change management, leadership and organizational culture. In a world where human interactions are key to success, emotional intelligence is not only a competitive advantage, but a fundamental need to build a different, innovative and sustainable company.

Talent of the Future

The concept of "future talent" is one that is redefining the way companies think about their workforce. In a world where change is the only constant, skills and competencies that were valuable yesterday may not be valuable tomorrow. Companies that want to be different and stand out in an increasingly competitive market must understand what type of talent they will need to meet the challenges of the future. Beyond technical skills, the talent of the future must be prepared for a dynamic work environment, characterized by constant innovation, rapidly evolving technology and the need to adapt to new ways of working.

To understand what it means to be part of the "talent of the future," we must first recognize that the future of work will not be like the past or the present. Global trends such as automation, artificial intelligence, remote work and the knowledge economy are radically changing the nature of employment. In this context, technical skills, although still important, are no longer sufficient. Companies are looking for employees who not only master today's tools, but are also able to quickly learn and adapt to tomorrow's tools. The ability to learn continuously, known as "lifelong learning", is becoming one of the most valued skills.

In addition to continuous learning, the talent of the future must be resilient and adaptable. Resilience, in this case, refers to the ability to overcome challenges, learn from failures, and move forward despite difficulties. In a world where economic crises, technological disruptions, and social changes can come out of nowhere, employees who can stay calm and find creative solutions are invaluable. Adaptability, on the other hand, is the ability to quickly adjust one's approach and mindset to new circumstances. Companies need people who can shift gears easily, who aren't scared by the unknown, and who see change as an opportunity rather than a threat.

Another fundamental aspect of the talent of the future is digital competence. Technology is at the heart of almost every industry, and those who cannot master digital tools will inevitably be left behind. However, digital competence goes beyond simply knowing how to use a computer or software. It involves the ability to understand how emerging technologies, such as artificial intelligence, automation and data analytics, can be leveraged to improve processes, make informed decisions and create value. The talent of the future must not only be able to use these technologies, but also understand their ethical and business implications.

Creativity and innovation are also key characteristics of the talent of the future. As routine and repetitive tasks are increasingly performed by machines, human skills, such as creativity, become more valuable. Companies look for employees who can think "outside the box," who can generate new ideas and approaches, and who are not afraid to challenge the status quo. Innovation is not just about creating new products or services, but also about finding more efficient and effective ways of doing things. In an environment where competition is fierce, the ability to innovate can be the difference between success and failure.

Furthermore, the talent of the future must be collaborative and able to work as a team. In the knowledge economy, work is no longer done in silos; Most projects require the collaboration of people with different skills and perspectives. The ability to work well with others, communicate effectively, and contribute to a team is essential. This includes not only internal collaboration within the company, but also the ability to work with external partners, customers and communities. Communication skills, both verbal and written, are essential in this regard. A team member who can express her own ideas clearly and listen to those of others has a significant advantage in any collaborative environment.

Global mindset is another important characteristic of future talent. In an increasingly interconnected world, companies often operate in multiple countries and cultures. Being globally minded means being aware of cultural differences, being able to work with people from different backgrounds, and being open to different ways of thinking and doing business. Diversity is not only an internal issue, but also an external one, and those who can navigate a globalized environment will be better prepared to succeed. This also implies a commitment to social responsibility and sustainability, as companies of the future will increasingly be forced to consider their impact on the world.

Leadership is another key aspect of future talent, and not just for those in management roles. Leadership in this context means taking the initiative, being proactive, and leading others toward achieving common goals. Companies look for people who don't wait for instructions, but rather identify opportunities and problems on their own and take action to address them. Leadership also involves the ability to inspire and motivate others, build strong relationships, and foster a positive work environment. In an environment where teams can be geographically dispersed and where remote work is increasingly common, effective leadership is more important than ever.

In addition to these competencies, the talent of the future must also be aligned with the company's values and mission. In an environment where employees seek a sense of purpose in their work, companies that can attract and retain the best talent are those that have a clear mission and strong values. Employees want to work for companies that reflect their own principles, that are committed to sustainability, inclusion and social responsibility. Therefore, companies that want to attract the talent of the future must ensure that their mission and values are not only communicated, but also lived in all areas of the organization.

A concrete example of what it means to be part of the talent of the future is the growing demand for skills in green technology and sustainability. As climate change and resource scarcity become pressing global issues, companies are looking for people who not only understand these challenges but can also develop innovative solutions to address them. This can include everything from renewable energy engineering to implementing sustainable business practices. Employees who can combine a deep understanding of sustainability with advanced technical skills will be in high demand in the coming years.

Finally, it is important to remember that the talent of the future is not only a matter of technical skills or specific competencies, but also of mentality. Companies that want to be different and successful in the future must cultivate a growth mindset in their workforce. This means being willing to learn, adapt and continually evolve. It means being open to new ideas and perspectives, and being willing to take risks and learn from mistakes. In an environment where change is inevitable, the ability to grow and evolve will be one of the most valuable competencies any employee can possess.

In short, the talent of the future is much more than a set of technical skills. It is a combination of resilience, adaptability, digital competence, creativity, collaboration, global mindset, leadership and alignment with company values. It is the ability to continually learn and grow, to face challenges with confidence, and to see change as an opportunity rather than a threat. Companies that recognize and cultivate this type of talent will be better prepared to meet the challenges of the future, to innovate and to thrive in a constantly evolving world. Ultimately, the talent of the future is the key to building a truly different company, capable of making a difference in the market and in society.

Paulette Durand

Flexible Organizational Structures

Flexible organizational structures are a concept that is transforming the way businesses operate in the modern world. Traditionally, organizations have been designed with rigid hierarchies and clear lines of command, where each employee has a well-defined role and reports to a specific superior. However, in a rapidly changing business environment, these structures can become outdated and limiting. Companies that want to be different and successful in the future need to adopt more agile and flexible structures, which allow them to quickly adapt to new opportunities and challenges.

A flexible organizational structure is, in essence, one that can change and adapt according to the needs of the business. Instead of following a rigid organizational chart, these structures allow teams to form and disintegrate based on ongoing projects. For example, instead of having separate departments that work independently, a flexible organization could form multidisciplinary teams to address specific problems or develop new products. These teams can be made up of people from different areas, such as marketing, product development, sales, and technology, who work together to achieve a common goal.

This approach has several advantages. First, it encourages innovation. When people with different skills and perspectives work together, new and creative ideas are more likely to emerge. Instead of being limited by the boundaries of a department, employees can collaborate more freely and leverage the collective knowledge of the organization. This is particularly important in an environment where innovation is key to staying competitive. Companies that adopt flexible structures can adapt quickly to changes in the market, launch new products faster and respond better to customer needs.

Another benefit of flexible organizational structures is the ability to respond more quickly to changes in the business environment. In a world where emerging technologies, market fluctuations and customer expectations can change from one moment to the next, companies need to be agile. Rigid, hierarchical organizations often have difficulty adapting to these changes because each decision must go through multiple levels of approval. Instead, a flexible structure allows teams to make decisions quickly and act quickly, giving them a significant competitive advantage.

Additionally, flexible structures can improve employee morale and satisfaction. In a traditional organization, employees often feel trapped in their roles, without much opportunity to grow or change. However, in a flexible organization, employees have the opportunity to work on different projects, learn new skills, and take on different roles based on their interests and abilities. This not only keeps employees motivated and engaged, but also allows them to develop a wide range of competencies, making them more valuable to the organization and to their future careers.

Flexibility can also help companies attract and retain talent. Younger generations of workers value autonomy, the opportunity to learn, and the ability to work on meaningful projects. Companies that can offer this type of environment are more attractive to the brightest and most motivated talent. Additionally, in a flexible environment, employees have more control over their work and can better balance their professional and personal responsibilities. This is especially important in a world where remote work and flexible working are becoming more common.

However, the adoption of flexible organizational structures is not without challenges. One of the biggest challenges is the need for clear and effective communication. In a flexible organization, where teams can form and dissolve quickly, it is crucial that everyone is aligned and clearly understands the goals and expectations. This requires a conscious effort to keep everyone informed and to ensure that information flows efficiently through the organization. Lack of communication can lead to misunderstandings, duplication of efforts, and ultimately inefficiency.

Another challenge is the need for leaders who can manage in a flexible environment. In a traditional organization, leaders often focus on managing tasks and making sure employees meet their responsibilities.

However, in a flexible organization, leaders should be facilitators rather than directors. This means they must be able to empower their teams, provide guidance when necessary, but also give them the space and autonomy to make decisions and act on their own. Leaders in flexible organizations must be comfortable with ambiguity and able to manage change effectively.

Additionally, flexible organizational structures require a different approach to performance management. In a traditional organization, performance is often measured based on an employee's ability to accomplish assigned tasks and achieve specific goals. However, in a flexible organization, performance is measured more by an employee's ability to adapt to new roles, to contribute to different projects, and to collaborate effectively with others. This requires a change in the way goals are set and how success is evaluated. Companies must develop performance metrics that reflect the dynamic and multidimensional nature of roles in a flexible organization.

Technology also plays a crucial role in supporting flexible organizational structures. Digital collaboration tools, such as project management platforms, communication apps, and remote work tools, are essential for keeping teams connected and coordinated. These tools allow teams to work together effectively, no matter where they are physically located. Additionally, technology can help companies track project progress, manage resources more efficiently, and ensure everyone is aligned with the organization's strategic goals.

It is important to note that flexibility does not mean lack of structure or chaos. In fact, for a flexible organization to function effectively, there must be a clear framework that guides how teams are formed, how decisions are made, and how resources are managed. This may include policies and procedures that establish how changes should be handled, how information should be communicated, and how conflicts should be resolved. A strong framework allows the organization to be flexible without losing control or consistency.

In short, flexible organizational structures are a response to the demands of the modern business environment. They allow companies to be more agile, innovative and receptive to change. At the same time, they offer employees more autonomy, development opportunities and greater job satisfaction. However, to successfully implement a flexible structure, companies must overcome challenges such as the need for clear communication, effective leadership, and an appropriate approach to performance management. By doing so, they can create an organization that is not only able to thrive in the present, but is also prepared to meet the challenges of the future.

Remote and Hybrid Work

Remote and hybrid work has ceased to be a passing trend and has become a permanent reality in the world of work. What was once an exception or a privilege reserved for a few, is today a common practice adopted by companies of all sizes and sectors. This change has radically transformed the way companies operate and how employees experience their work. In an environment where flexibility and adaptation are key to success, remote and hybrid work not only offer new opportunities, but also present unique challenges that companies must address to be truly different and successful.

Remote work, as the name suggests, is the ability for employees to perform their tasks from anywhere outside of the traditional office, whether from home, a coffee shop, a coworking space, or even while traveling. This type of work has become increasingly popular due to technological advances that allow people to stay connected and productive without needing to be physically present in one place. High-speed internet access, online collaboration tools, and video conferencing platforms have made it easier for teams to work together, regardless of geographic distance.

On the other hand, hybrid work combines the best of both worlds: it allows employees to split their time between working from home and working in the office. This offers greater flexibility, allowing people to take advantage of the benefits of working from home, such as convenience and time savings on the road, while maintaining the option to collaborate face-to-face with colleagues in the office when necessary. The hybrid model is particularly attractive because it recognizes that not all jobs or tasks are perfectly suited to a fully remote environment. There are times when in-person interaction is invaluable, and hybrid work allows companies to balance those needs.

One of the most obvious benefits of remote and hybrid work is the increase in flexibility for employees. This type of work setup allows people to better manage their time and balance their personal and professional responsibilities. The ability to work from home means that employees can, for example, care for their families, avoid long commutes, and organize their day so that they can be most productive at times that best suit them. This flexibility can lead to greater job satisfaction, which, in turn, can translate into lower turnover and employees who are more engaged and loyal to the company.

Another important benefit is the expansion of access to talent. Companies are no longer limited to hiring people who live near their offices. They can find and hire top talent, no matter where they are in the world. This is especially valuable in highly specialized fields, where finding people with the right skills can be a challenge. By enabling remote work, companies can access a much broader pool of candidates, which can be a significant competitive advantage. Additionally, by offering flexible work options, companies become more attractive to candidates seeking a better work-life balance.

However, remote and hybrid work also presents challenges that companies must manage carefully. One of the biggest challenges is maintaining company cohesion and culture when employees are not physically present in one location. Face-to-face interaction is an important part of how relationships are built and collaboration encouraged. When employees work remotely, it can be more difficult to create a sense of belonging and ensure everyone is aligned with company values and goals. To overcome this challenge, companies must be proactive in creating opportunities for social interaction and collaboration online, using digital tools to encourage open communication and teamwork.

Another challenge is performance management in a remote or hybrid environment. In the office, managers can observe their employees and offer feedback in real time. However, when employees work from home, managers must rely more on results and less on direct supervision. This requires a shift in mindset, moving from a focus on control and physical presence to one that focuses on trust and responsibility. Companies should establish clear performance metrics and expectations that allow employees to know what is expected of them, without the need for constant supervision. At the same time, managers must be available to support their teams and offer guidance when necessary.

Technology plays a critical role in the success of remote and hybrid work. Without the right tools, it can be difficult for employees to stay productive and connected. Companies should invest in communication and collaboration platforms that facilitate teamwork, as well as security solutions that protect sensitive company information when employees access it from remote locations. Additionally, it is important for companies to provide training and technical support to ensure that all employees can use these tools effectively. Technology can also help companies monitor the wellbeing of their employees, ensuring they do not feel isolated or disconnected when working from home.

Another important aspect to consider is the impact of remote and hybrid work on employees' mental health. While working from home can offer convenience and flexibility, it can also lead to feelings of isolation or disconnection if not managed properly. Lack of social interaction, difficulty disconnecting at the end of the day, and distractions at home are some of the challenges that can affect the mental health of remote employees. Companies should be aware of these risks and take steps to support the well-being of their employees. This may include promoting a culture of work-life balance, hosting online social activities, and offering mental health resources and services.

Remote and hybrid work can also have implications for companies' physical infrastructure. With fewer employees present in the office full-time, companies may reconsider their need for physical space. This could lead to a reduction in real estate costs, or a re-evaluation of office layout to better accommodate a hybrid environment. For example, instead of dedicating large areas to individual offices, companies could opt for shared workspaces, flexible meeting rooms and collaboration areas that adapt to the changing needs of employees. This approach can not only be more cost-efficient, but can also create a more dynamic work environment tailored to the needs of the team.

Finally, it is important to recognize that the success of remote and hybrid work depends largely on organizational culture. The companies that thrive in this environment are those that have built a culture of trust, flexibility and mutual support. This means that employees should feel empowered to make decisions and manage their own time, knowing that they have the support of their managers and colleagues. At the same time, companies must be transparent in their communication and be willing to adapt and learn as they navigate this new work landscape. Your company culture should reflect a commitment to the well-being and success of all your employees, regardless of where they work.

In short, remote and hybrid work is not just a passing trend, but an evolution in the way companies operate and how employees experience their work. It offers unprecedented flexibility, access to greater talent, and the opportunity to create a more balanced and productive work environment. However, it also presents challenges that require a conscious and strategic approach, from managing performance to maintaining company culture. Companies that successfully navigate these challenges will be better positioned to attract and retain talent, drive innovation, and remain competitive in an ever-changing world.

Purpose and Social Responsibility

In the past, business success was measured almost exclusively in terms of profits and economic growth. Companies focused on maximizing profits for their shareholders and expanding as quickly as possible, without paying much attention to the impact their operations could have on society or the environment. However, in recent years, this approach has begun to change significantly. Today, more and more companies recognize that to be truly successful, they must go beyond financial benefits and take an active role in creating a better world. This change in focus is reflected in the growing importance of purpose and social responsibility as central pillars of business strategy.

The purpose of a company is its reason for existence beyond generating profits. It is what motivates her, what guides her decisions and what gives meaning to her existence. A company with a clear purpose does not just focus on selling products or services, but on how those products or services can positively contribute to society. This purpose becomes the compass that directs all of the company's actions, from the way it treats its employees to how it interacts with its customers and the impact it has on the environment. A strong purpose not only attracts loyal customers, it also motivates employees, who feel part of something bigger than themselves.

Social responsibility, on the other hand, refers to the obligation that companies have to act ethically and contribute to the well-being of society. This means that companies cannot operate in a vacuum; They must be aware of how their activities affect people and the planet, and must take active steps to minimize any negative impacts. Social responsibility covers a wide range of practices, from respecting human rights and promoting diversity and inclusion, to reducing our carbon footprint and supporting local communities. In a world where consumers and employees are increasingly aware of social and environmental issues, social responsibility is no longer an option, but a necessity.

Purpose and social responsibility are closely interconnected. A company with a clear and authentic purpose is more inclined to genuinely assume its social responsibility. For example, if a company's purpose is to improve people's health, it is logical that it also commits to offering safe, high-quality products, promoting a healthy lifestyle, and minimizing its environmental impact in the production of those products. . This type of alignment between purpose and social responsibility not only benefits society, but also strengthens the company's brand, creating a deeper and lasting connection with its customers.

However, for purpose and social responsibility to be effective, they must be authentic. Companies cannot simply adopt them as a marketing gimmick or as a way to improve their public image. Today's consumers are extremely adept at detecting when a company is being disingenuous or simply following a trend. If a company declares that it has a purpose, but does not back up that declaration with concrete actions, it risks being seen as hypocritical, which can damage its reputation and alienate its customers and employees. Therefore, it is crucial that companies truly commit to their purpose and social responsibility, and demonstrate their commitment through tangible and measurable actions.

In addition to being the right thing to do, taking an approach based on purpose and social responsibility also makes sense from a business perspective. Research has shown that companies that focus on purpose and social responsibility tend to be more successful in the long term. Consumers are increasingly willing to support companies that share their values, and many people are willing to pay more for products and services from companies that align with their beliefs. Likewise, employees, especially younger generations, prefer to work for companies that have a clear purpose and demonstrate a genuine commitment to social responsibility. This means that companies with a strong focus on purpose and social responsibility can better attract and retain talent.

The role of companies in society has evolved. Today, companies not only have the opportunity, but also the responsibility, to address some of the world's most pressing challenges, such as climate change, social inequality, and lack of access to basic services such as health and safety. education. By adopting a clear purpose and assuming social responsibility, companies can be agents of positive change. For example, a company that commits to reducing its environmental impact can lead the transition towards a more sustainable economy, inspiring other companies to follow its example. Likewise, a company that focuses on gender equity can help close the gender gap in its industry, serving as a role model for other organizations.

To integrate purpose and social responsibility into the core of their business, companies must start by clearly defining their purpose. This means going beyond a simple mission statement and reflecting on the fundamental questions: Why do we exist as a company? What do we want to achieve in the world? How can we use our capabilities and resources to make a positive difference? Once the purpose has been defined, it is important to clearly communicate it to all levels of the organization and ensure that it is aligned with the company's daily strategies and operations. The purpose should not be an abstract idea, but a practical guide that informs every decision and action of the company.

Social responsibility must also be integrated into all areas of the company. This involves adopting policies and practices that reflect a commitment to ethical principles, sustainability and the well-being of society. For example, companies can implement diversity and inclusion policies to ensure that all employees, regardless of gender, race, or identity, have equal opportunities. They can adopt sustainable practices in their supply chains to reduce their environmental impact. They can collaborate with nonprofit organizations to support important causes in their communities. Social responsibility is not something that can be done in isolation; It must be an integral part of the company's culture and operations.

Measurement and transparency are key elements for successful purpose and social responsibility. Companies should set clear, measurable goals, and should monitor their progress on a regular basis. This not only helps the company stay on track, but also demonstrates to customers, employees, and other stakeholders that the company is committed to its values. Transparency is equally important; Companies must be open and honest about their successes and challenges on their path to fulfilling their purpose and social responsibility. This builds trust and strengthens the relationship between the company and its stakeholders.

Finally, it is important to recognize that purpose and social responsibility are not destinations, but continuous journeys. Society's expectations and global challenges are constantly evolving, and companies must be willing to adapt and continually improve their practices. This requires a learning mindset and a commitment to continuous improvement. Companies that take this approach will not only be better equipped to meet the challenges of the future, but will also be better positioned to create a lasting positive impact on society.

In conclusion, purpose and social responsibility are essential components of a truly different and successful company in the modern world. By adopting a clear purpose and genuinely embracing their social responsibility, businesses can not only prosper economically, but also contribute to the well-being of society and the planet. This approach is not only ethical, it is also strategic, attracting loyal customers, motivating employees and creating a brand that lasts over time. Companies that integrate purpose and social responsibility into the core of their business will be better prepared to meet the challenges of the future and to build a positive legacy that inspires generations to come.

Transparent and Authentic Communication

Communication is the heart of any company. It is the bridge that connects leaders with their employees, companies with their customers, and organizations with the outside world. Without effective communication, the best ideas can be lost, teams can fall apart, and companies can fail in their mission. In a world where trust and credibility are more important than ever, transparent and authentic communication has become a fundamental pillar for the success of any company that aspires to be different, innovative and responsible.

Transparency in communication means being clear, honest and open at all times. It's not just about sharing good news or successes, but also being candid about challenges, mistakes, and areas for improvement. Companies that practice transparency create an environment of trust, where employees feel valued and customers feel they are dealing with a genuine and ethical organization. This trust is crucial, as in a world full of information, people are increasingly able to identify when a company is being dishonest or evasive. Transparency, therefore, is not just a good practice; It is a necessity for any company that wants to earn the loyalty of its employees and customers.

Authenticity goes hand in hand with transparency. Being authentic means being faithful to the company's values, mission and purpose. It is showing the true personality of the organization, without pretensions or falsehoods. Authenticity is what allows a company to differentiate itself in a saturated market, where many organizations seem to say the same thing and promise the same thing. An authentic company is not afraid to show its humanity; acknowledges his failures, celebrates his achievements with humility, and always strives to improve. Authenticity is what makes communication meaningful and resonant, allowing the company to connect with people on a deeper level.

The combination of transparency and authenticity in communication has a powerful impact on organizational culture. When leaders communicate transparently, they establish a standard of honesty that is reflected throughout the company. Employees feel safer to express their opinions, share ideas, and speak out about issues without fear of retaliation. This creates a work environment where collaboration flourishes and where people feel empowered to contribute their best selves. Transparency also makes decision-making easier, as all team members have access to the same information and can work together toward a common goal.

For transparent and authentic communication to be effective, it must be constant and consistent. It cannot be something that is done from time to time or only when it is convenient. Companies must commit to communicating openly in all circumstances, even when the news is not the best. This includes being clear about the company's financial situation, about strategic changes or about difficult decisions that may affect employees. Consistency is key; If a company says one thing and does another, it will quickly lose credibility. Leaders must be the first to lead by example, demonstrating through their actions that they value transparency and authenticity.

A fundamental aspect of transparent and authentic communication is active listening. Communication is not just talking; It is also listening carefully and responding genuinely. Companies that listen to their employees, customers, and other stakeholders are better equipped to respond to their needs and concerns. Active listening involves creating channels where people can express their opinions and ensuring that those opinions are taken into account in decision-making. Not only does this improve satisfaction and engagement, but it can also be an invaluable source of ideas and innovation.

Companies must also be aware of the importance of empathy in communication. Being transparent and authentic does not mean being cold or indifferent; On the contrary, it requires an empathetic approach, where the feelings and perspectives of others are considered. For example, when communicating a difficult decision, such as staff cuts or significant changes to strategy, it is crucial to do so in a way that shows understanding and respect for those affected. Empathy in communication helps build stronger relationships and keep morale high, even in difficult times.

Transparent and authentic communication also has a direct impact on the relationship with customers. Today's consumers value honesty and are more likely to support companies that are open and frank about their practices and products. Companies that are transparent about how their products are made, how their operations are run, and how they treat their employees can earn customer loyalty more effectively than those that try to hide reality behind a facade of perfection. Authenticity in customer communication also creates an emotional connection, which can be a powerful competitive advantage.

Technology has changed the way companies communicate, and this has made transparency and authenticity even more important. With social media, blogs, and other digital platforms, companies have the ability to reach a global audience in real time. But with this ability comes the responsibility to be consistent and authentic across all channels. Companies that try to manipulate public perception or are inconsistent in their messaging open themselves up to immediate and potentially damaging criticism. On the other hand, companies that use technology to communicate openly and honestly can strengthen their reputation and create a loyal community of followers.

A common challenge companies face when trying to be transparent and authentic is the fear of vulnerability. Transparency often requires admitting mistakes or accepting that you don't have all the answers, which can be intimidating. However, it is important to remember that vulnerability is not a weakness; It is a strength. Companies that are able to show their human side, recognize their mistakes and learn from them, not only earn the respect of their employees and customers, but also establish a culture of continuous improvement. This attitude of humility and openness can be a significant advantage in a competitive business environment.

In short, transparent and authentic communication is essential to building a company that is not only successful, but also respected and admired. By adopting transparency and authenticity as guiding principles, companies can create an environment of trust, foster a positive organizational culture, and strengthen their relationships with customers and employees. In a world where trust is increasingly valuable, the ability to communicate clearly, honestly and empathetically is a key differentiator. Companies that master this art will be better positioned to meet the challenges of the future and to build lasting and meaningful relationships with all their stakeholders.

Paulette Durand

Customer Relations in the Digital Age

In the digital age, customer relationships have changed radically. Before, interactions between companies and their customers were quite simple and limited. A customer went to a store, bought a product, and their experience with the brand ended there. But with the arrival of the Internet, social networks, and mobile technology, this dynamic has evolved profoundly. Today, customers are more informed, more connected, and have higher expectations than ever. They understand that they have a voice and power, and they expect to be heard. This has transformed the way companies must approach customer relationships, forcing them to be more agile, more personalized, and more committed.

One of the most significant changes in the digital age is that customer relationships are no longer transactional; They are relational. This means that companies can no longer simply sell a product or service and end the relationship. Now, customers expect continued engagement. They want to be valued as individuals, not as simple buyers. This requires companies to invest in building long-term relationships, based on trust, loyalty and constant communication. Instead of focusing solely on sales, companies should focus their efforts on understanding their customers, anticipating their needs, and offering them solutions that truly add value to their lives.

Personalization is key in customer relationships in the digital age. Today's customers are accustomed to highly personalized experiences, thanks to the digital platforms they use in their daily lives, such as social networks, online stores, and streaming services. They expect companies to offer them products, services and communications that suit their individual preferences. Technology allows companies to collect and analyze large amounts of data about their customers, giving them the opportunity to personalize each interaction. However, this customization must be careful and respectful; Customers value their privacy, and companies must find the right balance between personalization and respect for personal information.

Social media has revolutionized the way companies interact with their customers.

These platforms offer a direct, real-time avenue to communicate with customers, which has changed the game for relationship management. Customers can now express their opinions, ask questions, and receive answers almost instantly. This has led to an expectation of faster and more efficient customer service. Companies that do not respond in a timely manner or do not properly handle online complaints may face negative consequences, as negative experiences can quickly spread in the digital world. On the other hand, companies that are responsive, respond with empathy, and solve problems effectively can earn the loyalty and respect of their customers.

The digital age has also democratized access to information. Customers can now easily research and compare products and services before making a purchasing decision. They can read reviews, see ratings, and consult other users' opinions in a matter of minutes. This means that companies no longer have full control over the information that customers receive about their products or services. Instead of trying to control the narrative, companies should embrace this transparency and ensure their products and services meet market expectations. Quality, honesty and consistency are more important than ever, as customers can quickly discover if a company does not live up to its promises.

In the digital age, customer loyalty has taken on a new meaning. It is no longer just about offering a good product or service, but about creating memorable and meaningful experiences that keep customers engaged with the brand. This can be achieved in several ways: personalized rewards programs, exclusive content, personalized interactions, and most importantly, exceptional customer service. Companies should strive to surprise and delight their customers at every opportunity, showing that they truly value them and appreciate their loyalty. Technology allows companies to create sophisticated loyalty programs that adapt to each customer's individual behaviors and preferences, which can be a key differentiating factor in a competitive market.

Customer feedback has become an invaluable tool in the digital age. With the ease of online surveys, reviews, and social media interactions, businesses have direct access to their customers' opinions like never before. This feedback can be used to improve products, adjust marketing strategies, and improve customer service. However, it is not enough to collect this information; Companies must act on it. Customers want to see that their opinions are heard and that their suggestions are taken into account. This not only improves the customer experience, but also strengthens the relationship between the company and its customers, creating a positive cycle of continuous improvement.

Speed is a critical factor in customer relationships in the digital age. Customers expect quick answers to their questions and immediate solutions to their problems. This has raised expectations for customer service, making agility a necessity. Companies must be prepared to respond in real time and to provide fast and effective solutions. This may involve the use of chatbots, automatic response systems, or customer service teams that are available 24 hours a day. However, it is important to remember that while speed is crucial, the quality of the interaction should not be sacrificed. Customers value speed, but they also appreciate friendly, professional and effective treatment.

Technology has allowed companies to globalize their operations and reach customers anywhere in the world. This presents both opportunities and challenges in customer relationship management. Companies must be aware of cultural differences and local expectations, and adapt their communication and service strategies accordingly. The ability to offer a personalized and relevant service in a global context is one of the keys to building strong and lasting relationships with customers in the digital age. This may require localizing content, adapting marketing strategies, and creating customer service teams that understand and respect the cultures and expectations of different markets.

Finally, it is important to recognize that customer relationships in the digital age are not static; They are constantly evolving. Technology continues to advance at a rapid pace, and with it, customer expectations change as well. Companies must be prepared to continually adapt, adopting new technologies, improving their processes, and keeping up with emerging trends. Innovation and flexibility are essential to maintaining strong customer relationships in a rapidly changing digital environment. Companies that are able to anticipate their customers' needs and adapt to these changes will be better positioned to thrive in the future.

In conclusion, customer relationships in the digital age require a proactive, personalized and customer experience-focused approach. Technology offers numerous opportunities to improve these relationships, but it also poses challenges that must be carefully managed. Transparency, personalization, speed, and adaptability are key to building and maintaining strong customer relationships in a digital world. Companies that master these skills will not only gain the loyalty of their customers, but will also be better prepared to face the challenges of the future and to take advantage of the opportunities presented by the digital age.

Collaboration and Co-Creation

In the modern business world, the idea of working in silos, where each department operates in isolation, no longer has a place. The companies that stand out today are those that have embraced collaboration and co-creation as central elements of their strategy. Collaboration goes beyond simple teamwork; It is a philosophy that encourages synergy between different areas, people and even organizations to achieve common goals. Co-creation, for its part, takes this idea one step further, inviting customers, partners, and other external actors to actively participate in the development of products, services and solutions. In this chapter, we will explore how collaboration and co-creation can transform the way companies operate, innovate and achieve success in a highly competitive environment.

Collaboration is the foundation on which modern organizations are built. Instead of relying on a rigid hierarchical structure where decisions and ideas come from the top down, today's successful companies foster a culture of teamwork where all members have the opportunity to contribute. This not only improves efficiency and productivity, but also enriches decision making by incorporating a diversity of perspectives and skills. Effective collaboration allows companies to respond more quickly and flexibly to market challenges and opportunities, creating an environment where innovation can flourish.

In this sense, technology has played a crucial role. Digital collaboration tools, such as online communication platforms, project management systems, and work-sharing applications, have removed geographic and time barriers, allowing teams to work together from anywhere in the world. This has opened the door to global collaboration, where companies can leverage talent and resources from diverse regions and cultures. However, technology alone does not guarantee effective collaboration; There needs to be an organizational culture that values cooperation, trust and transparency. Technology is an enabler, but it is the people who make collaboration successful.

Co-creation, on the other hand, is a natural extension of collaboration. It is a process in which companies invite their customers, partners, and other stakeholders to actively participate in the creation of value. This approach not only helps companies better understand their customers' needs and wants, but also allows customers to feel more involved and committed to the brand. Co-creation can take many forms, from co-developing new products to collaborating on marketing campaigns or improving existing services. By involving customers and other partners in these processes, companies not only generate more innovative ideas, but also build stronger, more loyal relationships.

A clear example of co-creation is the development of products through direct feedback from customers. Companies can use online platforms, surveys, and focus groups to gather ideas, suggestions, and opinions from their customers. This approach allows companies to create products and services that are aligned with what customers really want and need, reducing the risk of market failure. Additionally, when customers see that their opinions are valued and that their ideas are implemented, their brand loyalty increases significantly. Co-creation not only improves business results, but also strengthens the emotional connection between the company and its customers.

Another important aspect of co-creation is collaboration with other business partners. Instead of seeing other companies as competitors, many organizations are taking a collaborative approach, where they come together to create products, services or solutions that neither could develop alone. This form of collaboration, known as strategic alliances, allows companies to combine their resources, knowledge and skills to achieve a common goal. Whether it is a collaboration between companies in different industries, or between companies in the same sector, strategic alliances can be a powerful source of innovation and growth.

For collaboration and co-creation to be successful, it is essential that certain elements exist in the organizational culture. First, there must be a genuine commitment to openness and transparency. Employees and partners should feel comfortable sharing their ideas, even if they are unconventional or go against the grain. Diversity of thought is a key driver of innovation, and companies must foster an environment where different perspectives are celebrated and where people are encouraged to think creatively.

Secondly, trust is essential. Effective collaboration cannot occur in an environment where people feel unsafe or where mistrust exists between different teams or partners. Trust is built through open communication, mutual respect, and keeping commitments. Companies should strive to create relationships of trust both within the organization and with their external partners. This not only facilitates collaboration, but also creates an environment where people are more willing to take calculated risks and experiment with new ideas.

Communication also plays a vital role in collaboration and co-creation. It is essential that companies establish clear and effective communication channels that allow teams to share information, solve problems and coordinate their efforts efficiently. Communication must be fluid and constant, ensuring that everyone involved is aware of the progress, challenges and changes in the project. Furthermore, it is important that communication is two-way; Leaders must be willing to listen to and consider the ideas and concerns of others, which reinforces the sense of belonging and commitment of all participants.

Flexibility is another key component. In an environment of collaboration and co-creation, things rarely follow a linear path. Projects can change direction, priorities can be adjusted, and teams must be prepared to adapt to new circumstances. Companies that encourage flexibility and are willing to experiment with different approaches are more likely to discover innovative solutions and respond effectively to market challenges. Flexibility also means being open to the evolution of ideas, allowing the contributions of different actors to shape and improve the final result.

Collaboration and co-creation are not without challenges. Coordinating the efforts of different teams, departments, and partners can be complicated, especially when there are differences in culture, goals, or expectations. It is crucial that companies address these challenges proactively, establishing clear processes, defined roles and mechanisms to resolve conflicts. The key to overcoming these obstacles lies in maintaining focus on the common goal and working together toward a shared vision. Companies that manage to integrate collaboration and co-creation into their organizational DNA are better positioned to innovate, adapt and thrive in an ever-changing business environment.

In short, collaboration and co-creation are essential to building companies that not only survive, but thrive in today's business world. These approaches enable organizations to make the most of available talent and resources, while fostering innovation and strengthening relationships with customers and partners. By creating a culture that values cooperation, transparency, trust, communication and flexibility, companies can unlock new opportunities for growth and success. In a world where change is the only constant, the ability to collaborate and co-create becomes a key differentiator for companies seeking to lead in their respective industries.

Global Expansion with Responsibility

In an increasingly interconnected world, global expansion has become an almost inevitable strategy for many companies seeking to grow and reach new markets. Globalization offers countless opportunities, from access to a broader customer base to the ability to diversify revenue streams and reduce risks. However, expanding globally is not simply a matter of replicating local success in other countries. It requires a deep understanding of cultural, legal, economic and social differences, as well as a firm commitment to social and environmental responsibility. In this chapter, we will explore how companies can undertake responsible global expansion, balancing growth with a positive impact on communities and the environment.

The first step in responsible global expansion is research and preparation. Before entering a new market, companies should do a thorough analysis of local conditions. This includes understanding the culture, customs, values and expectations of consumers. What works in one country or region will not necessarily work in another. Adaptation is key.

Companies must be willing to adjust their products, services and marketing strategies to align with local needs and preferences. This approach not only increases the chances of success, but also demonstrates a respect for local cultures, which is essential for building long-lasting, trusting relationships.

Another crucial aspect of global expansion is legal and regulatory compliance. Each country has its own set of laws and regulations that businesses must comply with to operate. These may include rules on labor rights, environmental protection, trade, taxes and corporate responsibility. Ignoring or minimizing the importance of compliance can have serious consequences, from financial penalties to damage to a company's reputation. Companies that expand responsibly globally understand the importance of working within each country's legal framework and acting with integrity in all their operations. This not only protects the company from legal risks, but also reinforces its commitment to ethics and sustainability.

Environmental sustainability is an essential component of responsible global expansion. As companies grow and expand into new markets, their environmental footprint can also increase. It is crucial that companies adopt sustainable practices that minimize their impact on the environment. This may include the use of renewable energy, the reduction of carbon emissions, proper waste management, and the implementation of efficient and clean production processes. Additionally, companies must consider the environmental impact of their operations on local communities and take steps to protect ecosystems and natural resources. Sustainability is not only a moral obligation, but can also be a key factor for long-term success, as consumers and communities increasingly value companies that demonstrate a commitment to protecting the planet.

Social responsibility also plays a central role in global expansion. Companies must consider how their operations affect local communities. This includes not only job creation, but also respect for labor rights, fair treatment of employees, and contribution to the economic and social development of the areas where they operate. Responsible companies strive to be good corporate citizens, investing in initiatives that benefit communities, such as education, health, and infrastructure development. Furthermore, they must ensure that their business practices do not exploit or harm local populations, but instead empower them and provide them with opportunities to improve their quality of life.

Transparency and ethics are fundamental in responsible global expansion. Companies must be clear and honest in their communications, both with their employees and with their customers, partners and the communities in which they operate. This includes reporting on its labor practices, its environmental impact, and its corporate governance policies. Transparency builds trust, and trust is essential to building strong relationships in a new market. Additionally, companies must adhere to the highest ethical standards in all their operations, avoiding practices such as corruption, bribery, and exploitation. Business ethics is not only the basis of social responsibility, but also protects the company from reputational and legal risks.

Global expansion must also consider the economic impact on local communities. While a company's entry into a new market can bring benefits, such as job creation and economic development, it can also have negative effects if not managed responsibly. For example, the entry of large corporations into local markets can displace small businesses and negatively affect local economies. Companies that responsibly expand globally must be aware of these potential impacts and take steps to support local economies. This can include collaborating with local suppliers, investing in local skills development, and creating economic opportunities that benefit rather than harm communities.

Cultural adaptation is another crucial factor in global expansion. Companies that operate in multiple countries must be aware of cultural differences and be willing to adapt their products, services and communication strategies to these differences. This does not mean simply translating marketing materials or products, but understanding and respecting the values, beliefs and customs of each market. Cultural adaptation demonstrates genuine respect for local communities and can be a key factor for success in a new market. Additionally, companies that adopt a global and multicultural perspective are often better prepared to innovate and compete in a diverse global environment.

Collaborating with local partners is also an effective strategy for responsible global expansion. By working with local businesses, organizations can benefit from the knowledge and experience of those who already understand the market. This not only facilitates adaptation to local conditions, but also strengthens relationships with communities and contributes to local economic development. Strategic partnerships with local companies can help organizations navigate the regulatory, cultural and economic environment of a new market, increasing the likelihood of success and minimizing risks.

Finally, responsible global expansion requires a long-term vision. It's not just about making quick profits, but about building a sustainable and respected presence in new markets. Companies must be patient, willing to invest in developing strong relationships, and maintain an ongoing commitment to social and environmental responsibility. This long-term approach not only benefits the company, but also contributes to the well-being of the communities and the sustainable development of the regions in which it operates.

In short, responsible global expansion is a balance between growth and ethics. Companies that aspire to expand globally must do so in a way that respects and benefits local communities, protects the environment, and operates with the highest standards of transparency and ethics. By taking a responsible approach to their global expansion, companies not only maximize their chances of success, but also contribute positively to the world in which they operate. This approach is not only a smart strategy, but also a moral obligation in a world where companies have the power to influence the well-being of people and the planet.

Paulette Durand

Sustainable Finance and Long-Term Profitability

In today's business world, the focus on finance has evolved significantly. It's no longer just about maximizing short-term profits or showing impressive numbers in quarterly reports. Now, companies are recognizing the importance of sustainable finances and long-term profitability as keys to lasting success. This shift in mindset involves not only how revenue is generated, but also how resources are managed, capital is invested, and risk is mitigated. In this chapter, we will explore how sustainable finance can guide businesses toward a more prosperous and responsible future, balancing economic needs with social and environmental responsibilities.

Sustainable finance is based on the idea that companies must consider not only financial benefits, but also the impact their decisions have on the environment and society. This means that investment and spending decisions are not made solely on the basis of immediate economic returns, but also consider the long-term effects on the natural environment and communities. This approach is not only ethical, but also makes business sense, as consumers, investors and employees are increasingly interested in supporting companies that demonstrate a commitment to sustainability.

A fundamental component of sustainable finance is responsible investing. This involves directing capital towards projects, companies and initiatives that promote environmental sustainability and social well-being. For example, companies may choose to invest in renewable energy, clean technologies, or conservation initiatives, rather than in industries that have a high negative environmental impact. Responsible investing also includes supporting companies that maintain high labor standards and contribute positively to the communities where they operate. By making investment decisions based on environmental, social and governance (ESG) criteria, companies can not only generate financial returns but also promote positive change in the world.

Efficient resource management is also key to sustainable finance. Companies that focus on sustainability understand that how they use their resources, from financial capital to materials and energy, has a direct impact on their long-term profitability. Resource efficiency not only reduces costs, but also minimizes waste and environmental impact. For example, implementing cleaner production practices and optimizing energy and water use can result in significant savings while reducing the company's ecological footprint. This approach creates a virtuous cycle where sustainability and profitability reinforce each other.

Another important aspect of sustainable finance is risk mitigation. In a world increasingly affected by climate change, social crises and economic volatility, companies must be aware of the risks that these realities represent for their business. Sustainable finance advocates proactive management of these risks, including identifying potential threats, planning for different scenarios, and implementing strategies that reduce the company's vulnerability. For example, a company that depends on natural resources can mitigate risks by investing in sustainable management practices of said resources, guaranteeing their future availability. In this way, companies not only protect their profitability, but also contribute to the resilience of ecosystems and communities.

Transparency and accountability are essential components in sustainable finance. Companies need to be open about their financial practices and how these align with their sustainability commitments. This includes the disclosure of information on investments, expenses, and results in terms of sustainability. Transparency not only strengthens trust among shareholders, employees and customers, but also allows the company to evaluate its progress and make adjustments when necessary. By being responsible and transparent in their financial approach, companies can build a solid reputation that distinguishes them in an increasingly competitive and conscious market.

Commitment to long-term profitability is another pillar of sustainable finance. Instead of seeking quick profits, sustainable businesses focus on strategies that allow them to grow consistently and responsibly over time. This can involve investments in innovation, talent development, and building strong relationships with customers and communities. Long-term profitability is also achieved by creating sustainable value, that is, generating products and services that are not only profitable, but also have a positive impact on the world. This long-term approach protects the company against market fluctuations and allows it to build a solid foundation for the future.

An interesting aspect of sustainable finance is how it can attract a new generation of investors and consumers. Today, there is growing investor interest in supporting companies that are not only seeking financial returns, but are also committed to creating a positive impact on the world. Investment funds and stock portfolios that focus on ESG criteria are on the rise, and companies that demonstrate a strong commitment to sustainability are more likely to attract these types of investments. Additionally, consumers are increasingly willing to support companies that share their values and work to make the world a better place. By aligning themselves with these trends, companies can not only ensure their financing and growth, but also strengthen their brand and their relationship with their customers.

Financial education also plays a crucial role in implementing sustainable finances. Companies should train their employees and leaders in the principles of financial sustainability, ensuring they understand the importance of balancing economic objectives with social and environmental commitments. Sustainable financial education helps employees make more informed decisions aligned with the company's mission, which in turn drives overall performance and profitability. Additionally, by fostering a culture of financial sustainability, companies can inspire their employees to be advocates for positive change both inside and outside the organization.

Sustainable finance also requires a focus on innovation. As companies seek to balance profitability with sustainability, innovation becomes a key tool. This may include the development of new products and services that meet the demands of a more conscious and responsible market, as well as the implementation of processes and technologies that improve efficiency and reduce environmental impact. Innovation can also help companies find new ways to generate revenue that are aligned with their sustainability principles, which in turn can open new opportunities for growth and expansion in emerging markets.

Finally, it is important to recognize that sustainable finance is not a destination, but rather an ongoing journey. Companies must be willing to adapt and evolve as market conditions and consumer expectations change. This requires a continuous improvement mindset and a commitment to reviewing and adjusting strategies to ensure they remain effective and aligned with sustainability goals. Companies that take this approach are better equipped to meet the challenges of the future and to continue to thrive in a world that increasingly values responsibility and sustainability.

In conclusion, sustainable finances and long-term profitability are not just trends, but fundamental pillars for success in the modern business environment. Companies that integrate sustainability into their financial strategy not only achieve profitable growth, but also contribute to a more equitable and sustainable future for all. This balanced approach between profitability and responsibility is what will allow companies to not only survive, but thrive in a world where social and environmental expectations are higher than ever. Sustainable finance is ultimately an investment in the future, not only of the company, but also of the planet and society as a whole.

Measuring Success in Different Companies

In the era of traditional business, success was primarily measured in terms of financial profits, sales growth, and shareholder value. However, in the context of "Different Companies", these indicators, although still important, are no longer the only parameters that define success. The companies of the future are changing the narrative, looking for more comprehensive and meaningful ways to evaluate their performance. These new metrics not only consider economic aspects, but also social, environmental and human impact. In this chapter, we will explore how to measure success in these innovative companies, taking a more holistic approach that truly reflects what it means to thrive in the 21st century.

The first step to measuring success in a Different Company is to redefine what "success" means. For many of these organizations, success is not limited to the numbers on the bottom line. Instead, it is about creating value that is sustainable over the long term, benefiting all stakeholders, including employees, customers, communities and the environment. This means that, in addition to traditional financial indicators, companies must adopt metrics that reflect their social and environmental impact, as well as the satisfaction and well-being of their employees and customers.

One of the key indicators in measuring success in Different Companies is social impact. This refers to the company's ability to generate positive change in society. Companies can measure their social impact in several ways, including the number of jobs created, the improvement in the quality of life of the communities in which they operate, or the contribution to social causes such as education, health and equality. Some companies take a more structured approach, using tools such as the Social Impact Index (SII) or sustainability reports that quantify and qualify their contribution to social well-being. By making this impact a key indicator of success, companies demonstrate that their mission goes beyond profits and that they are committed to the positive development of society.

Environmental impact is another fundamental pillar in measuring success. In a world where sustainability has become a global priority, companies must evaluate their ecological footprint and actively work to reduce it. This includes measuring and reporting carbon emissions, consumption of resources such as water and energy, and waste management. Leading sustainability companies are going further, setting ambitious goals to reduce their environmental impact, such as achieving carbon neutrality or eliminating the use of single-use plastics in their operations. These goals not only improve the company's reputation, but also contribute to the preservation of the planet for future generations, which is a crucial indicator of success in a Different Company.

In addition to social and environmental impact, employee well-being is an essential component in measuring success. Different Companies understand that their employees are not just a resource, but the heart and soul of the organization. Therefore, measuring success also involves assessing employee satisfaction, happiness, and overall well-being. This can be done through satisfaction surveys, employee retention and turnover analysis, and monitoring the mental and physical health of employees. Companies that prioritize the well-being of their workers not only create a more positive work environment, but also experience higher levels of productivity, creativity and innovation, which is a clear reflection of their success.

Customer satisfaction remains a vital indicator, but in Different Companies, it goes beyond simply measuring sales or positive reviews. It's about building long-term relationships based on trust, transparency and authenticity. Companies can measure this by analyzing customer loyalty, customer lifetime value (CLV), and Net Promoter Score (NPS), which measures customers' willingness to recommend the company to others. However, it is also important to consider customer opinions and suggestions to continually improve and adapt products and services to their changing needs. Companies that succeed in cultivating a loyal and satisfied customer base are building a solid foundation for sustained success.

Another key metric in measuring success in Different Companies is continuous innovation. In a world where change is the only constant, companies must be in a state of constant evolution and adaptation. Measuring innovation is not just about counting the number of new products launched or patents registered, but about evaluating how these innovations are positively impacting the company and society. This includes the implementation of new technologies, the improvement of internal processes, and the company's ability to quickly adapt to market trends and customer needs. Companies that maintain a culture of continuous innovation are those that can face the challenges of the future with confidence and creativity.

Commitment to purpose is another crucial factor in measuring success. Different Companies are often driven by a purpose greater than the simple desire for profit. This purpose may be related to improving people's lives, protecting the environment, or promoting equity and social justice. Measuring success involves evaluating how the company is achieving its purpose and what impact it is having on the world. This commitment to a higher purpose not only inspires employees and engages customers, but also gives meaning and direction to all of the company's activities. Organizations that remain true to their purpose over time are the ones that truly leave a significant mark on the world.

Additionally, it is important to consider sustainable growth as an indicator of success. Different Companies do not seek rapid growth at any cost, but growth that is sustainable and responsible in the long term. This means expanding in a way that maintains a balance between economic, social and environmental needs. Companies can measure this sustainable growth by analyzing their long-term profitability, their ability to maintain a competitive position in the market, and their success in diversifying and adapting their revenue sources. Sustainable growth is a reflection of the strength and long-term vision of the company.

Finally, collaboration and alliances are important indicators of success in Different Companies. These organizations understand that working collaboratively with others – whether businesses, non-governmental organizations, governments or communities – can amplify their positive impact. Measuring success in this context involves evaluating the quality and impact of these alliances, as well as the company's ability to work synergistically with others. Companies that manage to build and maintain effective strategic alliances can access new resources, markets and knowledge, allowing them to advance their mission and strengthen their position in the market.

In short, measuring success in Different Companies requires a broader and deeper approach than simple financial analysis. These companies are redefining what it means to be successful, focusing not only on profitability, but also on social and environmental impact, and the well-being of all stakeholders. By adopting these more comprehensive metrics, Different Companies not only ensure their long-term sustainability and relevance, but also contribute significantly to the well-being of society and the planet. This holistic approach to measuring success is what will allow these companies to thrive in the future and leave a lasting legacy of accountability and leadership.

9 798822 743267